SPORTS

32 Choices, One Winner!

By Rob "Stats" Guerrera

Andrews McMeel
PUBLISHING®

To my wife, Erin, and my children, Thomas and Diana. You are everything.
—Rob

Andrews McMeel Publishing
a division of Andrews McMeel Universal
1130 Walnut Street, Kansas City, Missouri 64106

www.andrewsmcmeel.com

23 24 25 26 27 RLP 10 9 8 7 6 5 4 3 2 1

ISBN: 978-1-5248-8884-8

Editor: Erinn Pascal
Art Director: Tiffany Meairs
Production Editor: Meg Utz
Production Manager: Tamara Haus

ATTENTION: SCHOOLS AND BUSINESSES
Andrews McMeel books are available at quantity discounts with bulk purchase
for educational, business, or sales promotional use. For information, please e-mail
the Andrews McMeel Publishing Special Sales Department:
sales@amuniversal.com.

Whether it's played with a ball, a puck, or a racket, sports games and tournaments delight audiences around the world. But which sport is the best? What players in each sport stand above the rest?

In your hands is a very special sports-themed Bracketivity book. Within these pages, you'll be able to pick your favorite thing in each category. But it's not just a "pick and go" situation—you'll have to fill each bracket to determine your winner!

Think about each answer carefully, because it determines your next round of brackets. Or go with your gut feeling—really, there are no wrong answers! And at the end of the book, you'll even get to make your own Bracketivities to share with family and friends.

Just remember—have fun!

Football is the most popular sport in the United States. What's your favorite National Football League (NFL) team?

Kansas City Chiefs

Philadelphia Eagles

Philadelphia Eagles

San Francisco 49ers

Buffalo Bills

San Francisco 49ers

San Francisco 49ers

San Francisco 49ers

Minnesota Vikings

Minnesota Vikings

Cincinnati Bengals

Minnesota Vikings

Dallas Cowboys

Dallas Cowboys

Los Angeles Chargers

San Francisco 49ers

Baltimore Ravens

New York Giants

New York Giants

New York Giants

Jacksonville Jaguars

Jacksonville Jaguars

Miami Dolphins

New York Giants

Seattle Seahawks

Detroit Lions

Detroit Lions

Detroit Lions

Pittsburgh Steelers

Pittsburgh Steelers

Washington Commanders

BRACKETIVITY EXAMPLE

Here's an example **Bracketivity** that's filled out. It's what your author would pick. Don't worry—if you disagree, you'll get to fill out your own on the next page.

Tennessee Titans

New England Patriots

Tampa Bay Buccaneers

New York Jets

New England Patriots

New York Jets

Green Bay Packers

New York Jets

Tennessee Titans

Tennessee Titans

Tennessee Titans

Carolina Panthers

New Orleans Saints

Cleveland Browns

New Orleans Saints

Las Vegas Raiders

Las Vegas Raiders

Atlanta Falcons

Las Vegas Raiders

Las Vegas Raiders

Los Angeles Rams

Denver Broncos

Los Angeles Rams

Las Vegas Raiders

Arizona Cardinals

Indianapolis Colts

Arizona Cardinals

Chicago Bears

Chicago Bears

Houston Texans

Chicago Bears

San Francisco 49ers
Winner

Football is the most popular sport in the United States. What's your favorite National Football League (NFL) team?

Kansas City Chiefs

Philadelphia Eagles

Buffalo Bills

San Francisco 49ers

Minnesota Vikings

Cincinnati Bengals

Dallas Cowboys

Los Angeles Chargers

Baltimore Ravens

New York Giants

Jacksonville Jaguars

Miami Dolphins

Seattle Seahawks

Detroit Lions

Pittsburgh Steelers

Washington Commanders

Tampa Bay Buccaneers

New England Patriots

Green Bay Packers

New York Jets

Tennessee Titans

Carolina Panthers

Cleveland Browns

New Orleans Saints

Atlanta Falcons

Las Vegas Raiders

Denver Broncos

Los Angeles Rams

Indianapolis Colts

Arizona Cardinals

Houston Texans

Chicago Bears

Winner

Football players have had some fun nicknames over the years. Of these, which nickname is your favorite?

"Iron" Mike Ditka

Charles "Peanut" Tillman

Anthony "Booger" McFarland

"Marion the Barbarian" Marion Barber III

Daryl "Moose" Johnston

Jerome "The Bus" Bettis

"Muscle Hamster" Doug Martin

"Pocket Hercules" Maurice Jones-Drew

Damon "Snacks" Harrison

"The Galloping Ghost" Red Grange

"Ironhead" Craig Heyward

"Concrete Charlie" Chuck Bednarik

"The Minister of Defense" Reggie White

"Neon" Deion Sanders

"Sweetness" Walter Payton

"Mean" Joe Greene

Elroy "Crazylegs" Hirsch

William "The Refrigerator" Perry

"The Kansas Comet" Gale Sayers

Elbert "Ickey" Woods

"Megatron" Calvin Johnson

"Legatron" Greg Zuerlein

Billy "White Shoes" Johnson

Ken "The Snake" Stabler

"Captain Comeback" Roger Staubach

"Broadway" Joe Namath

"The Nigerian Nightmare" Christian Okoye

"Joe Cool" Joe Montana

"Honey Badger" Tyrann Mathieu

"Beast Mode" Marshawn Lynch

Ed "Too Tall" Jones

Dick "Night Train" Lane

Winner

What's your favorite sport to play?

Baseball

Cricket

Basketball

Karate

Football

Rugby

Golf

Pool

Soccer

Surfing

Hockey

Figure Skating

Tennis

Pickleball

Lacrosse

Field Hockey

Esports

Ping-Pong

Volleyball

Fencing

Boxing

Cheerleading

Bowling

Fishing

Archery

Track and Field

Swimming

Gymnastics

Horse Racing

Rowing

Snowboarding

Skiing

Winner

The quarterback is the leader of the offense in football. Who is your favorite quarterback?

Joe Montana

Steve Young

Peyton Manning

Eli Manning

John Elway

Terry Bradshaw

Bart Starr

Warren Moon

Kurt Warner

Jim Kelly

Philip Rivers

Tony Romo

Troy Aikman

Fran Tarkenton

Dan Marino

Tom Brady

Patrick Mahomes

Josh Allen

Lamar Jackson

Aaron Rodgers

Justin Herbert

Russell Wilson

Dak Prescott

Aaron Rodgers

Cam Newton

Jalen Hurts

Kyler Murray

Matthew Stafford

Derek Carr

Joe Burrow

Trevor Lawrence

Kirk Cousine

Winner

Imagine that you scored the final point needed in an important sports game. What are you most excited to do next?

3:0

Go to a Theme Park

Go to the Mall

Go on a Trip to Paris

Do a Bunch of TV Interviews

Do a Bunch of Radio Interviews

Pose for Photos with Fans

Sign Autographs for Fans

Take a Nap

Hug My Family

Play Another Game

Go Camping

Eat Tons of Candy

Record a Video

Write in My Diary

Shake Hands with the Other Team

Hug My Team

Throw a Party

Go to My Favorite Restaurant

High-Five My Team

Party with Friends

Eat a Cake

Do Volunteer Work

Go to a Parade

Re-Watch the Moment on TV

Do a Fortnite Dance Move

Play Video Games

Stay Up Late

Eat Ice Cream

Have a Karaoke Party

Be Interviewed for the Newspaper

Write My Memoir

Buy New Sporting Gear

Winner

In football, wide receivers catch passes from the quarterback. Who is your favorite wide receiver?

98

Jerry Rice

Terrell Owens

Randy Moss

Larry Fitzgerald

Isaac Bruce

Tim Brown

Steve Largent

Lance Alworth

Calvin Johnson

Don Maynard

Don Hutson

Cris Carter

Steve Smith Sr.

Reggie Wayne

Lynn Swann

Raymond Berry

DeAndre Hopkins

Davante Adams

Julio Jones

Justin Jefferson

Stefon Diggs

Cooper Kupp

Odell Beckham Jr.

Ja'Marr Chase

CeeDee Lamb

DK Metcalf

A.J. Brown

Deebo Samuel

DeVonta Smith

Mike Evans

Antonio Brown

Jaylen Waddle

Winner

Of these, who is your favorite soccer player of all time?

Lionel Messi

Alex Morgan

Kylian Mbappé

Neymar

Kevin De Bruyne

Megan Rapinoe

Mohamed Salah

Sergio Ramos

Luka Modrić

Harry Kane

Antoine Griezmann

Achraf Hakimi

Toni Kroos

Alphonso Davies

Casemiro

Trent Alexander-Arnold

Cristiano Ronaldo

Robert Lewandowski

Sadio Mané

Mia Hamm

Karim Benzema

Virgil van Dijk

Zlatan Ibrahimović

Vini Jr.

Abby Wambach

Bernardo Silva

Alexia Putellas

Adriana Leon

Nichelle Prince

Pelé

Luis Suárez

Son Heung-min

Winner

Of these choices, which is your favorite professional cheerleading team?

Kansas City Chiefs

Philadelphia Eagles

Buffalo Bills

San Francisco 49ers Gold Rush

Minnesota Vikings

Cincinnati Ben-Gals

Dallas Cowboys

Los Angeles Charger Girls

Baltimore Ravens

New York Giants

Jacksonville ROAR

Miami Dolphins

Seahawks Dancers

Detroit Lions

Pittsburgh Steelerettes

Command Force

Tampa Bay Buccaneers

New England Patriots

Green Bay Packers

New York Jets Flight Crew

Tennessee Titans

Carolina Topcats

Cleveland Browns

New Orleans Saintsations

Atlanta Falcons

Las Vegas Raiderettes

Denver Broncos

Laker Girls

Indianapolis Colts

Arizona Cardinals

Houston Texans

Chicago Honey Bears

Winner

Imagine you're about to play a basketball game, but the basketball is missing. What do you think would make the funniest replacement for a basketball?

A Frisbee

A Potato

A Whoopee Cushion

A Video Game Controller

A Pair of Sneakers

A Roll of Toilet Paper

My Dirty Underwear

A Bunch of Toenail Clippings

Slime

Moldy Leftovers

A Baseball

The Coach's Whistle

A Taco

A Box of Spaghetti

A Disco Ball

A Drone

An Avocado

A Whole Tree

A Pair of Ice Skates

The Coach's Cell Phone

A Pot of Flowers

A Whole Pizza

A Soccer Ball

Pom-Poms

A Litter Box

A Wig

A Laser Sword

A Set of Car Keys

A Surfboard

A Meatball

A Rubber Chicken

A Teddy Bear

Winner

Baseball was once referred to as America's pastime. It's been popular since the 1700s! Which team name is your favorite?

(We even threw in two old ones from teams that aren't around anymore!)

New York Yankees

Boston Red Sox

Toronto Blue Jays

Tampa Bay Rays

Baltimore Orioles

Chicago White Sox

Kansas City Royals

Cleveland Guardians

Minnesota Twins

Detroit Tigers

Texas Rangers

Houston Astros

Oakland Athletics

Los Angeles Angels

Seattle Mariners

Montreal Expos

Chicago Braves

New York Mets

Miami Marlins

Philadelphia Phillies

Washington Nationals

Pittsburgh Pirates

Milwaukee Brewers

Chicago Cubs

St. Louis Cardinals

Cincinnati Reds

Los Angeles Dodgers

Arizona Diamondbacks

San Diego Padres

Colorado Rockies

San Francisco Giants

Washington Senators

Winner

Nicknames for baseball players are some of the most famous in all of sports. What's your favorite Major League Baseball (MLB) player nickname?

"Oil Can" Dennis Boyd

"The Big Hurt" Frank Thomas

"The Big Unit" Randy Johnson

"Hammerin'" Hank Aaron

"The Splendid Splinter" Ted Williams

"Crime Dog" Fred McGriff

"Mr. October" Reggie Jackson

"Shoeless" Joe Jackson

"The Wizard of Oz" Ozzie Smith

"Charlie Hustle" Pete Rose

"The Iron Horse" Lou Gehrig

"The Man of Steal" Rickey Henderson

"The Say Hey Kid" Willie Mays

"The Sultan of Swat" Babe Ruth

"The Human Rain Delay" Mike Hargrove

"The Heater from Van Meter" Bob Feller

"The Millville Meteor" Mike Trout

"El Niño" Fernando Tatís Jr.

"Polar Bear" Pete Alonso

"Boomstick" Nelson Cruz

"Sho Time" Shohei Ohtani

"Flying Squirrel" Jeff McNeil

"Bam Bam" Bryce Harper

"Cookie" Carlos Carrasco

"Mad Max" Max Scherzer

"Mr. Smile" Francisco Lindor

"The Claw" Clayton Kershaw

"Sandman" Mariano Rivera

"Big Papi" David Ortiz

"Thor" Noah Syndergaard

"Joey Bats" Jose Bautista

"Kung Fu Panda" Pablo Sandoval

Winner

Every baseball field looks a little different. What is the coolest baseball stadium?

(Including a couple that no longer exist!)

Fenway Park (Boston, MA)

Oriole Park at Camden Yards (Baltimore, MD)

Yankee Stadium (New York, NY)

Tropicana Field (St. Petersburg, FL)

Rogers Centre (Toronto, Canada)

Progressive Field (Cleveland, OH)

Kauffman Stadium (Kansas City, MO)

Comerica Park (Detroit, MI)

Guaranteed Rate Field (Chicago, IL)

Target Field (Minneapolis, MN)

Globe Life Field (Arlington, TX)

Minute Maid Park (Houston, TX)

T-Mobile Park (Seattle, WA)

Oakland Coliseum (Oakland, CA)

Angel Stadium (Anaheim, CA)

The Polo Grounds (New York, NY)

Citi Field (Queens, NY)

Citizens Bank Park (Philadelphia, PA)

LoanDepot Park (Miami, FL)

Nationals Park (Washington, D.C.)

Truist Park (Atlanta, GA)

Great American Ball Park (Cincinnati, OH)

Busch Stadium (St. Louis, MO)

American Family Field (Milwaukee, WI)

Wrigley Field (Chicago, IL)

PNC Park (Pittsburgh, PA)

Oracle Park (San Francisco, CA)

Petco Park (San Diego, CA)

Coors Field (Denver, CO)

Chase Field (Phoenix, AZ)

Dodger Stadium (Los Angeles, CA)

Shea Stadium (Queens, NY)

Winner

Imagine that you are on a travel baseball team. Which city are you most excited to play in?

Kansas City, MO

Nashville, TN

St. Louis, MO

Chicago, IL

Montreal, Canada

Portland, OR

Boston, MA

Charleston, SC

Atlanta, GA

Austin, TX

San Francisco, CA

Seattle, WA

Tampa, FL

Minneapolis, MN

San Antonio, TX

Savannah, GA

Orlando, FL

Los Angeles, CA

New York, NY

Portland, ME

Washington, D.C.

Miami, FL

Cincinnati, OH

Milwaukee, WI

New Orleans, LA

Dallas, TX

Denver, CO

Raleigh, NC

Detroit, MI

Las Vegas, NV

Memphis, TN

San Diego, CA

Winner

Write in your own:

With the following prompt, fill in your own bracketivity!

Imagine that you're on a volleyball team and need someone to play with. Write in 32 of your friends' names, and then see who wins the spot!

Winner

If you could time travel and interview any of these athletes from history, who would you want to meet most?

Jim Thorpe

Wilt Chamberlain

Jackie Robinson

Lou Gehrig

Jesse Owens

Mickey Mantle

Cy Young

Stan Musial

Kobe Bryant

Rocky Marciano

Ted Williams

Yogi Berra

Flo Hyman

Bill Russell

Reggie White

Sonja Henie

Babe Ruth

Muhammad Ali

Walter Payton

Sammy Baugh

Joe DiMaggio

Roberto Clemente

Sam Snead

Hank Aaron

Ty Cobb

Jimmie Foxx

Forrest Gregg

Wilma Rudolph

Ben Hogan

Otto Graham

Dick "Night Train" Lane

Walter Johnson

Winner

Of these, which sport would you LEAST want to partake in?

Cheerleading

Baseball

Gymnastics

Cross-Country

Basketball

Handball

Dodgeball

Fencing

Figure Skating

Cycling

Ice Hockey

Football

Golf

Hang Gliding

Soccer

Surfing

Bowling

Boxing

Foosball

Field Hockey

Curling

Kung Fu

Skydiving

Archery

Cricket

Kayaking

Badminton

Horseback Riding

Kickball

Mountain Biking

Pickleball

Rugby

Winner

You're going surfing! In which place would you most like to go surfing?

Mykonos, Greece

Aruba

Ko Samui, Thailand

San Sebastian, Spain

Gold Coast, Australia

Sardinia, Italy

Bali, Indonesia

Palawan, Philippines

Hanalei Bay, Hawaii

Sicily, Italy

Hossegor, France

Buxton, North Carolina

Ipanema Beach, Brazil

Rincón, Puerto Rico

Cornwall, England

Montanita, Ecuador

Winner

Castaway Island, Fiji

Honolulu, Hawaii

Olympos, Turkey

Malibu, California

Crete, Greece

La Digue, Seychelles

Horseshoe Bay, Bermuda

Okinawa, Japan

Tahiti, French Polynesia

Mallorca, Spain

Cancún, Mexico

Grand Cayman, Cayman Islands

Tulum, Mexico

Varadero Beach, Cuba

Miami, Florida

Oahu, Hawaii

What's your favorite song to sing at a sports game?

"We Will Rock You" – Queen

"Sandstorm" – Darude

"Y.M.C.A." – Village People

"Centerfield" – John Fogerty

"Born to Run" – Bruce Springsteen

"Welcome to the Jungle" – Guns N' Roses

The Star-Spangled Banner

"Whoomp! (There It Is)" – Tag Team

"Lose Yourself" – Eminem

Monday Night Football Theme

"We're Not Gonna Take It" – Twisted Sister

"Are You Ready for Some Football?" – Hank Williams Jr.

"Celebration" – Kool & the Gang

"Another One Bites the Dust" – Queen

"A Moment Like This" – Kelly Clarkson

"Kung Fu Fighting" – Carl Douglas

"We Are the Champions" – Queen

"Eye of the Tiger" – Survivor

"Rock 'n' Roll" – Gary Glitter

"Don't Stop Believin'" – Journey

"Let's Get It Started" – Black Eyed Peas

"Sweet Caroline" – Neil Diamond

"Who Let the Dogs Out" – Baha Men

"New York, New York" – Frank Sinatra

"Talking Baseball" – Terry Cashman

"It Takes Two" – Rob Base

"Hit the Road Jack" – Ray Charles

"Party in the USA" – Miley Cyrus

"All Star" – Smash Mouth

"Wild Thing" – X

"Take Me Out to the Ballgame"

"Enter Sandman" – Metallica

Winner

Some impressive athletes get scholarships to college so that they can play for the school's team while also getting their degree.

If you were offered a scholarship to one of these colleges, which one would you most want to attend?

University of Florida

Harvard University

Colgate University

Columbia University

Princeton University

University of Miami

Tulane University

University of Arizona

Cornell University

Brown University

University of Illinois

Air Force Academy

Duke University

Alabama State University

University of North Carolina at Chapel Hill

Yale University

Clemson University

Boston College

Vanderbilt University

Buffalo State University

Auburn University

Purdue University

Texas A&M University

Florida State University

University of Missouri

Stanford University

University of Michigan

Georgia Tech

Northwestern University

Indiana University

University of California, Irvine

University of California, Davis

Winner

Which basketball team is your favorite?

Milwaukee Bucks

Toronto Raptors

Boston Celtics

Chicago Bulls

Philadelphia 76ers

Indiana Pacers

Cleveland Cavaliers

Washington Wizards

New York Knicks

Orlando Magic

Brooklyn Nets

Charlotte Hornets

Atlanta Hawks

Detroit Pistons

Miami Heat

Harlem Globetrotters

Denver Nuggets

New Orleans Pelicans

Memphis Grizzlies

Oklahoma City Thunder

Sacramento Kings

Dallas Mavericks

Phoenix Suns

Utah Jazz

Los Angeles Clippers

Portland Trail Blazers

Golden State Warriors

Houston Rockets

Los Angeles Lakers

San Antonio Spurs

Minnesota Timberwolves

Indianapolis Olympians

Winner

Guards in the National Basketball Association (NBA) usually handle the ball more than any other position. Of these, who is your favorite guard?

Magic Johnson

Gary Payton

Oscar Robertson

Walt Frazier

Jerry West

Nate Archibald

Isaiah Thomas

Pete Maravich

John Stockton

Tony Parker

Steve Nash

Lenny Wilkens

Bob Cousy

Dave Bing

Jason Kidd

Reggie Miller

23

Steph Curry

Anthony Edwards

Chris Paul

Klay Thompson

Russell Westbrook

Jaylen Brown

Damian Lillard

Donovan Mitchell

Kyrie Irving

Bradley Beal

James Harden

Zach LaVine

Kobe Bryant

Devin Booker

Michael Jordan

Dwyane Wade

Winner

The Women's National Basketball Association (WNBA) began in 1997 and is home to the best players in the world. Who is your favorite WNBA player?

Diana Taurasi

Brittney Griner

Tamika Catchings

Tina Charles

Cynthia Cooper

Lindsay Whalen

Maya Moore

Angel McCoughtry

Lisa Leslie

Cappie Pondexter

Sheryl Swoopes

Nneka Ogwumike

Lauren Jackson

Becky Hammon

Sue Bird

Rebekkah Brunson

Candace Parker

Penny Taylor

Sylvia Fowles

Swin Cash

Elena Delle Donne

Candice Dupree

Breanna Stewart

Chamique Holdsclaw

Yolanda Griffith

Taj McWilliams-Franklin

Seimone Augustus

DeLisha Milton-Jones

Tina Thompson

Deanna Nolan

Katie Smith

Ticha Penicheiro

Winner

The National Hockey League (NHL) is the second oldest sports league in North America. Which NHL team do you think is the best?

Boston Bruins

Carolina Hurricanes

Toronto Maple Leafs

New Jersey Devils

Tampa Bay Lightning

New York Rangers

Florida Panthers

New York Islanders

Buffalo Sabres

Pittsburgh Penguins

Ottawa Senators

Washington Capitals

Detroit Red Wings

Philadelphia Flyers

Montreal Canadiens

St. Louis Blues

Colorado Avalanche

Vegas Golden Knights

Dallas Stars

Edmonton Oilers

Minnesota Wild

Los Angeles Kings

Winnipeg Jets

Seattle Kraken

Nashville Predators

Calgary Flames

Columbus Blue Jackets

Vancouver Canucks

Arizona Coyotes

San Jose Sharks

Chicago Blackhawks

Anaheim Ducks

Winner

In hockey, defenders back up the forward line and are responsible for stopping the other team's offense. Who is your favorite defender?

Bobby Orr

Chris Chelios

Ray Bourque

Scott Stevens

Larry Robinson

Rod Langway

Paul Coffey

Larry Murphy

Chris Pronger

Brian Leetch

Denis Potvin

Pierre Pilote

Nicklas Lidström

Scott Niedermayer

Doug Harvey

Brad Park

Cale Makar

Devon Toews

Adam Fox

Morgan Rielly

Roman Josi

Rasmus Dahlin

Aaron Ekblad

Dougie Hamilton

Jaccob Slavin

Erik Karlsson

Miro Heiskanen

Josh Morrissey

Charlie McAvoy

Quinn Hughes

Victor Hedman

Brandon Montour

Winner

Write in your own:

With the following prompt, fill in your own bracketivity!

A love for watching sports can take you all over the planet. Write down everything on your sports "bucket list" and then decide which one you're most excited about. A bucket list is all the cool things you want to do in your life!

Winner

In hockey, goalies are the last line of defense and can keep their team in a game all by themselves. If they do that, people say they are "standing on their head." Who is your favorite goalie?

Patrick Roy

Bernie Parent

Martin Brodeur

Georges Vezina

Dominik Hasek

Turk Broda

Ken Dryden

Clint Benedict

Bill Durnan

Billy Smith

Glenn Hall

Gump Worsley

Jacques Plante

Frank Brimsek

Terry Sawchuk

George Hainsworth

Linus Ullmark

Stuart Skinner

Jake Oettinger

Joonas Korpisalo

Alexandar Georgiev

Marc-André Fleury

Juuse Saros

Pyotr Kochetkov

Andrei Vasilevskiy

Vitek Vanecek

Connor Hellebuyck

Jeremy Swayman

Filip Gustavsson

Frederik Andersen

Ilya Sorokin

Ilya Samsonov

Winner

Picking your favorite player in each sport is one thing, but now we're going to make things a bit tougher. Who is your favorite player in ANY sport?

Patrick Mahomes

Josh Allen

Micah Parsons

Megan Rapinoe

Steph Curry

Kevin Durant

LeBron James

Giannis Antetokounmpo

Shohei Ohtani

Mike Trout

Aaron Judge

Abby Wambach

Connor McDavid

Sidney Crosby

Billie Jean King

Cristiano Ronaldo

Breanna Stewart

A'ja Wilson

Caitlin Clark

Angel Reese

Serena Williams

Venus Williams

Novak Djokovic

Roger Federer

Tara Lipinski

Phil Mickelson

Sha'Carri Richardson

Scottie Scheffler

Alex Morgan

Simone Biles

Lionel Messi

Kylian Mbappé

Winner

Write in your own:

With the following prompt, fill in your own bracketivity!

There are a lot of great team names out there.
Fill in this bracket with all the cool things
you would consider naming a team yourself.
Then see which one wins!

Winner

Many stadiums sell special foods to fans watching the game. In Seattle, you can eat toasted grasshoppers while watching the Mariners play baseball. What's your favorite thing to eat while watching a game?

Potato Chips

Tortilla Chips

Pretzels

Cheesy Crackers

Marshmallows

Sour Candy

Trail Mix

Pork Rinds

Kettle Corn

Graham Crackers

Vanilla Wafers

Chocolate Bars

Apples

Hummus and Pita

Turkey Legs

Cotton Candy

French Fries

Beef Jerky

Churros

Sliders

Hot Dogs

Fish and Chips

Cuban Sandwiches

Pizza Slices

Nachos

Garden Salads

Cheesesteaks

Sloppy Joes

Chicken Sandwiches

Lollipops

Toasted Grasshoppers

Ice Cream Sundaes

Winner

The International Olympic Committee (IOC) recognizes chess as a sport. What's a board game or tabletop game that you love the MOST?

Monopoly

Scrabble

Checkers

Settlers of Catan

Ticket to Ride

Risk

Guess Who?

Sequence

Backgammon

Rummikub

Mouse Trap

Trouble

Cards Against Humanity

Operation

Jenga

Table Shuffleboard

Chess

Chutes and Ladders

Dungeons & Dragons

Sorry!

The Game of Life

Candyland

Clue

Scattergories

Blokus

Battleship

Tic-Tac-Toe

Hungry Hungry Hippos

Uno

Yahtzee

Trivial Pursuit

Pretty Pretty Princess

Winner

Write in your own:

With the following prompt, fill in your own bracketivity!

Live sports accounted for 94 of the 100 most viewed things on TV in 2022. Write in all of your favorite things to watch on television (including sports games), then see which one is your favorite of ALL TIME!

Winner

The Olympics are international sports competitions that started almost 3,000 years ago! What is your favorite event in the Summer Olympics?

Swimming

Diving

Archery

Fencing

Rowing

Sailing

Tennis

Ping-Pong

Judo

Karate

Boxing

Hockey

Pentathlon

Rugby

Soccer

Badminton

Gymnastics

Trampoline

Weightlifting

Marksmanship

100 Meter Dash

Hurdles

Golf

Skateboarding

Water Polo

Wrestling

Basketball

Discus

Baseball

Softball

Equestrian

Sport Climbing

Winner

One of the most popular Winter Olympics sports is figure skating. Of these, who is your favorite figure skater or ice dancer?

Tara Lipinski

Marina Anissina

Nathan Chen

Yuna Kim

Sasha Cohen

Michelle Kwan

Kurt Browning

Karen Chen

John Curry

Dorothy Hamill

Tessa Virtue

Sergei Grinkov

Mao Asada

Oksana Baiul

Scott Moir

Kamila Valieva

Yuzuru Hanyu

Nancy Kerrigan

Johnny Weir

Anastasia Mishina

Sui Wenjing

Scott Hamilton

Katarina Witt

Brian Boitano

Sonja Henie

Carol Heiss

Sarah Hughes

Ekaterina Gordeeva

Brian Orser

Jayne Torvill

Surya Bonaly

Paul Wylie

Winner

Paris was chosen to host the 2024 Summer Olympics, Los Angeles will host the 2028 Olympics, and Brisbane, Australia, will host the 2032 games. Which place do you hope will host the Summer Olympics next?

Athens, Greece

St. Louis, Missouri

Stockholm, Sweden

Berlin, Germany

Antwerp, Belgium

Mexico City, Mexico

Calgary, Canada

Salt Lake City, Utah

Rome, Italy

Amsterdam, Netherlands

Tokyo, Japan

Helsinki, Finland

Sarajevo, Bosnia and Herzegovina

London, United Kingdom

Oslo, Norway

Melbourne, Australia

Sydney, Australia

Turin, Italy

Moscow, Russia

Seoul, South Korea

Nagano, Japan

Barcelona, Spain

Cairo, Egypt

Grenoble, France

Vancouver, Canada

Miami, Florida

Innsbruck, Austria

Bogotá, Colombia

Rio de Janeiro, Brazil

Beijing, China

Montreal, Canada

St. Moritz, Switzerland

Winner

Write in your own:

With the following prompt, fill in your own bracketivity!

Sports can be emotional. Write down 32 things you say when you're frustrated and see which one you'd shout during a game or activity!

Winner

Golf was invented more than 600 years ago! Who is your favorite golfer of all time?

Tiger Woods

Bobby Jones

Jack Nicklaus

Sam Snead

Arnold Palmer

Byron Nelson

Phil Mickelson

Tom Watson

Rory McIlroy

Jordan Spieth

Gary Player

Brooks Koepka

Ben Hogan

Jon Rahm

Walter Hagen

Scottie Scheffler

Annika Sörenstam

Lilia Vu

Michelle Wie West

Grace Kim

Karrie Webb

Nelly Korda

Juli Inkster

Georgia Hall

Nancy Lopez

Céline Boutier

Inbee Park

Jin Young Ko

Mickey Wright

Hannah Green

Betsy King

Ruoning Yin

Winner

Sports have also inspired some of the most beloved movies of all time. What's your favorite sports movie?

The Sandlot

Hoosiers

Little Giants

McFarland, USA

Air Bud

Underdogs

Field of Dreams

Back of the Net

The Natural

The Big Green

Rudy

Everyone's Hero

Space Jam

Brink!

Mighty Ducks

Dreamer

Miracle

Searching for Bobby Fischer

Kicking and Screaming

Million Dollar Arm

Invincible

Soul Surfer

Rookie of the Year

The Express

A League of Their Own

The Rookie

Karate Kid

Cool Runnings

Little Big League

Angels in the Outfield

Secretariat

Remember the Titans

Winner

The National Association for Stock Car Auto Racing (NASCAR) hosts some exciting race car tournaments.
Which of these vehicles do you think would be the fastest in a race?

Race Car

Police Car

Helicopter

Airplane

Bulldozer

Submarine

Blimp

Hot-Air Balloon

Fire Truck

Wagon

Tank

Hovercraft

Eighteen-Wheeler

Fan Boat

School Bus

Steamroller

Motorcycle

Jetpack

Scooter

Bicycle

Tractor

Sled

Cement Mixer

Dump Truck

Golf Cart

Go-Kart

Mobile Home

Snowmobile

Jet Ski

Hang Glider

Speed Boat

Cruise Ship

Winner

Which of these athletes do you think would be most likely to win an arm-wrestling match?

Kobe Bryant

Dave Bautista

Michael Phelps

Muhammad Ali

Venus Williams

Naomi Osaka

David Beckham

Gareth Bale

Stephen Curry

Tom Brady

Aaron Rodgers

Kristi Yamaguchi

Neymar

Virat Kohli

Lionel Messi

Hulk Hogan

LeBron James

Dwayne "The Rock" Johnson

Babe Ruth

Megan Rapinoe

Marshawn Lynch

James Rodríguez

Paul Pogba

Serena Williams

Ryan Lochte

Michelle Kwan

Michael Jordan

Cristiano Ronaldo

Kevin Durant

Shaquille O'Neal

Zlatan Ibrahimović

Marcelo Vieira Jr.

Winner

Write in your own:

With the following prompt, fill in your own bracketivity!

Which athlete would you most want
to have dinner with?

Winner

Esports are video games played by professionals. Hundreds of millions of people play esports every year. Of these, what's your favorite video game?

Mario Kart

Overwatch

Fortnite

Splatoon

Animal Crossing

Super Smash Bros.

Untitled Goose Game

Mega Man Legends

Minecraft

Piggy

Bendy and the Ink Machine

Hello Neighbor

Five Nights at Freddy's

Among Us

Spyro

Cuphead

Rocket League

Horizon Zero Dawn

The Legend of Zelda

Tetris

Madden NFL

Kingdom Hearts

PGA Tour

Roblox

FIFA

Ratchet & Clank

Sea of Thieves

Pokémon

Stray

Super Mario Odyssey

Kirby

Wii Sports

Winner

Which animal do you think would make the best athlete?

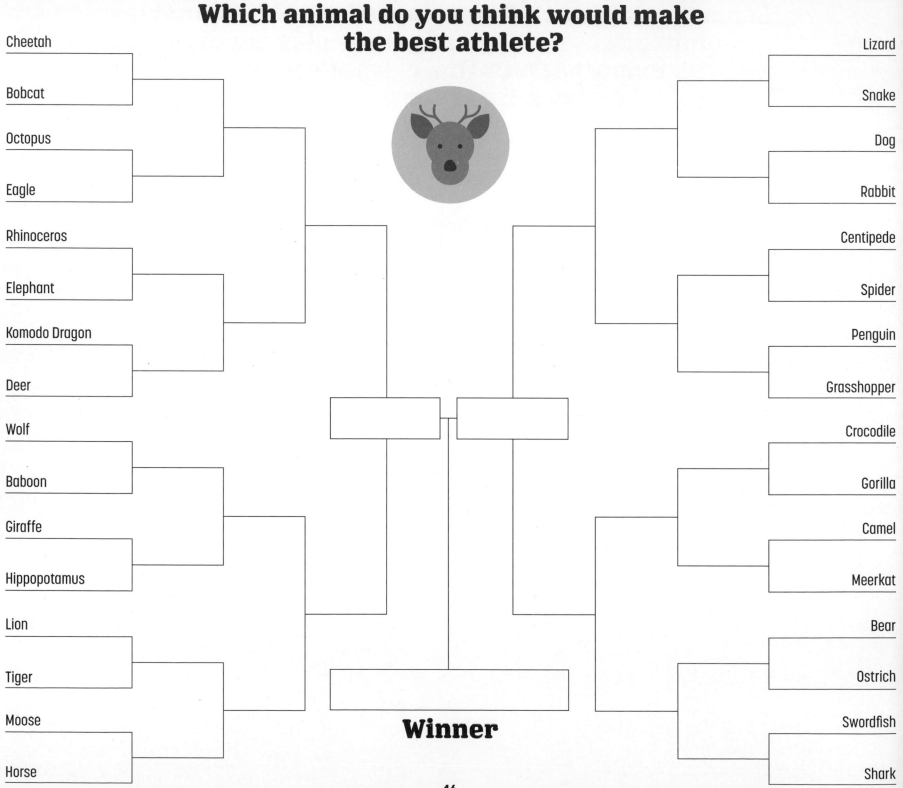

Cheetah

Bobcat

Octopus

Eagle

Rhinoceros

Elephant

Komodo Dragon

Deer

Wolf

Baboon

Giraffe

Hippopotamus

Lion

Tiger

Moose

Horse

Lizard

Snake

Dog

Rabbit

Centipede

Spider

Penguin

Grasshopper

Crocodile

Gorilla

Camel

Meerkat

Bear

Ostrich

Swordfish

Shark

Winner

Every sport has rules, and the penalties for breaking those rules can have some really interesting names. Which of these penalties sound the most serious to you?

Unsportsmanlike Conduct

Chop Block

Horse-Collar Tackle

Intentional Grounding

Icing

Slashing

Spearing

Gross Misconduct

Balk

Interference

Sign-Stealing

Obstruction

Offsides

Handball

Foot Foul

Delay of Game

Goaltending

Charging

Traveling

Flagrant Foul

Head-Butting

Butt-Ending

Dissent

Fault

Match Fixing

Solicitation

Point Penalty

Lane Violation

Deduction

Hindrance

Too Many Players on the Field

Double Dribble

Winner

Imagine you're designing your team's uniforms. What color or pattern do you hope is on it?

Brick Red

Cheetah Print

Navy

Gray

Dark Yellow

Forest Green

Zebra Stripes

Rainbow Polka Dots

Neon Green

Pale Yellow

Dark Purple

Bubblegum Pink

Metallic Silver

Black-and-White Stripes

Periwinkle

Dark Brown

Yellow Polka Dots

Beige

Metallic Gold

Turquoise

Rainbow Tie-Dye

Carnation Pink

Sky Blue

Apricot

Bright Orange

Peach

Lavender

Light Green

Tiger Stripes

White

Snakeskin

Green Floral

Winner

Many teams have mascots that cheer on the players and (hopefully) bring the team luck. Which mascot is your favorite?

Phillie Phanatic

Slamson the Lion

Steely McBeam

Crunch the Wolf

Benny the Bull

Stuff the Magic Dragon

Big Red

San Diego Chicken

Wally the Green Monster

Go the Gorilla

Mariner Moose

Mick E. Moose

Pirate Parrot

Jazz Bear

Mr. Met

Hugo

Jaxson de Ville

Pat Patriot

Sir Purr

Sourdough Sam

Artie the Fighting Artichoke

Uga

Bananas T. Bear

Boss Hog

Stanford Tree

Brutus Buckeye

Otto the Orange

Sparty

Barrelman

Gritty

Harvey the Hound

Fin the Whale

Winner

Which country do you think will take home the most gold medals in the next Summer Olympics?

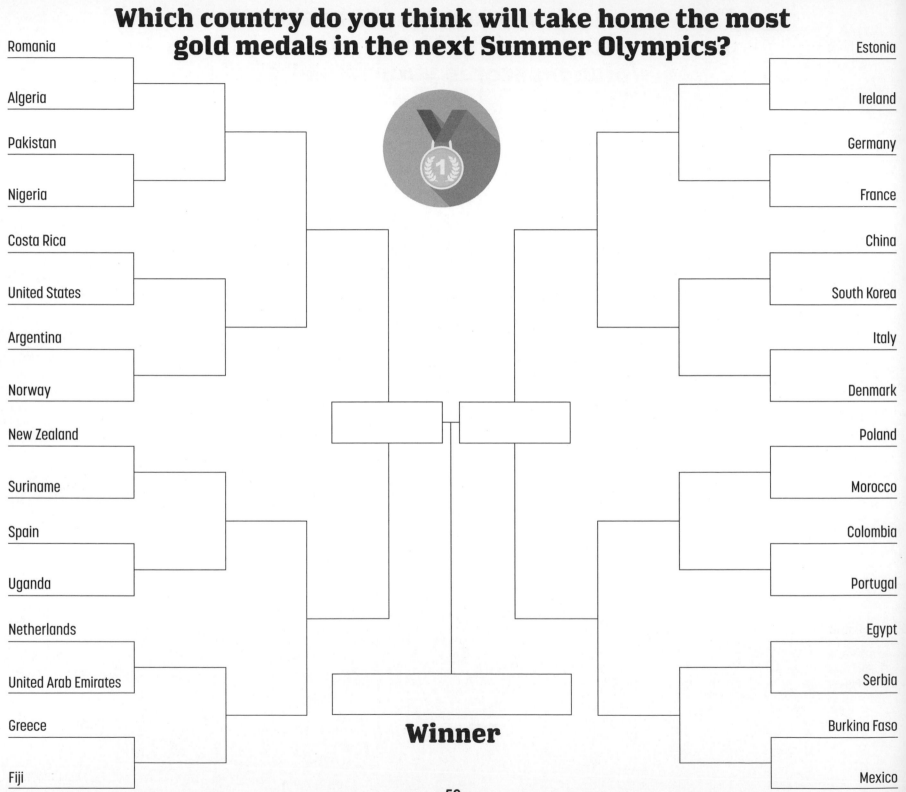

Romania

Algeria

Pakistan

Nigeria

Costa Rica

United States

Argentina

Norway

New Zealand

Suriname

Spain

Uganda

Netherlands

United Arab Emirates

Greece

Fiji

Estonia

Ireland

Germany

France

China

South Korea

Italy

Denmark

Poland

Morocco

Colombia

Portugal

Egypt

Serbia

Burkina Faso

Mexico

Winner

Of these, which country do you think will win the next FIFA World Cup?

Canada

Australia

Barbados

Germany

Nicaragua

Colombia

Dominican Republic

United States

Belgium

Morocco

Ethiopia

Brazil

Grenada

Croatia

Bangladesh

Mexico

Winner

Austria

Andorra

Costa Rica

Bermuda

Bhutan

France

Belize

China

England

Egypt

Guatemala

Venezuela

India

Italy

Lesotho

Lebanon

For your birthday party this year, you're taking all of your friends out to play a sport. Which sport sounds the most fun?

Rollerblading

Karate

Esports

Ballet

Foosball

Chess

Tae Kwon Do

Salsa Dancing

Ice Hockey

Bowling

Laser Tag

Gymnastics

Tennis

Ping-Pong

Mini Golf

Darts

Ice Skating

Archery

Tap Dancing

Parachuting

Bobsledding

Basketball

Boxing

Horseback Riding

Frisbee

Beach Volleyball

Go-Karting

Canoeing

Soccer

Rock Climbing

Trampolining

Kickball

Winner

52

Athletes must always stay hydrated!
What's the best drink to sip on after a game?

Water

Chocolate Milk

Fruit Punch

Vitamin Water

Orange Juice

Blueberry Smoothie

Matcha

Watermelon Juice

Mango Lassi

Pepsi

Gatorade

Peanut Butter Smoothie

Club Soda

Sparkling Water

Root Beer

Mountain Dew

Iced Tea

Pink Lemonade

Kombucha

Dr Pepper

Ginger Ale

Cream Soda

Shirley Temple

Coconut Water

Apple Juice

Strawberry Smoothie

Pineapple Juice

Chicken Broth

Chocolate Milkshake

Almond Milk

Green Tea

Coca-Cola

Winner

Pretend that you're the commentator of a sports game or competition! Which sport do you hope it is?

Basketball

Baseball

Figure Skating

Ice Hockey

Tennis

Badminton

Golf

Auto Racing

Cycling

Triathlon

Lacrosse

Track and Field

Horseback Riding

Karate

Surfing

Rugby

Soccer

Ice Dancing

Esports

Cheerleading

Ballet

Dodgeball

Bobsledding

Cricket

Water Polo

Chess

Baseball

Volleyball

Wrestling

Fencing

Swimming

Curling

Winner

Good news—you're getting something signed by your favorite player. What is it?

Ice Skates

Handheld Video Game Console

Bowling Ball

Paddle

Mountain Bike

Surfboard

Baseball

Boxing Glove

Billiard Ball

Photograph

Trophy

Action Figure

Comic Book

Baseball Bat

Sneakers

Reusable Water Bottle

Soccer Cleats

Hockey Stick

Their Memoir

Chess Set

Dartboard

Goggles

Poster

Medal

Baseball Mitt

Tennis Racket

Golf Club

Race Car

Hockey Puck

Football Helmet

Basketball

Trading Card

Winner

Water sports are played—you guessed it—on or in the water. Which water sport would you want to partake in FIRST this summer?

Boat Racing

Kiteboarding

Rowing

Parasailing

Fishing

Jet Skiing

Rafting

Kayaking

River Trekking

Surfing

Wake Boarding

White Water Rafting

Water Aerobics

Synchronized Diving

Water Polo

Water Skiing

Cable Skiing

Canoeing

Kneeboarding

Stone Skipping

Yachting

Triathlon

Free Diving

Underwater Football

Dragon Boat Racing

Rafting

Swimming

Paddleboarding

Skimboarding

Water Volleyball

Snorkeling

Underwater Rugby

Winner

Now it's your turn!

Now that you're a pro at Bracketivities, it's time to come to the plate!

Turn the page and make your own. You can also use this page to jot down any notes you have.

Winner

Winner

Winner

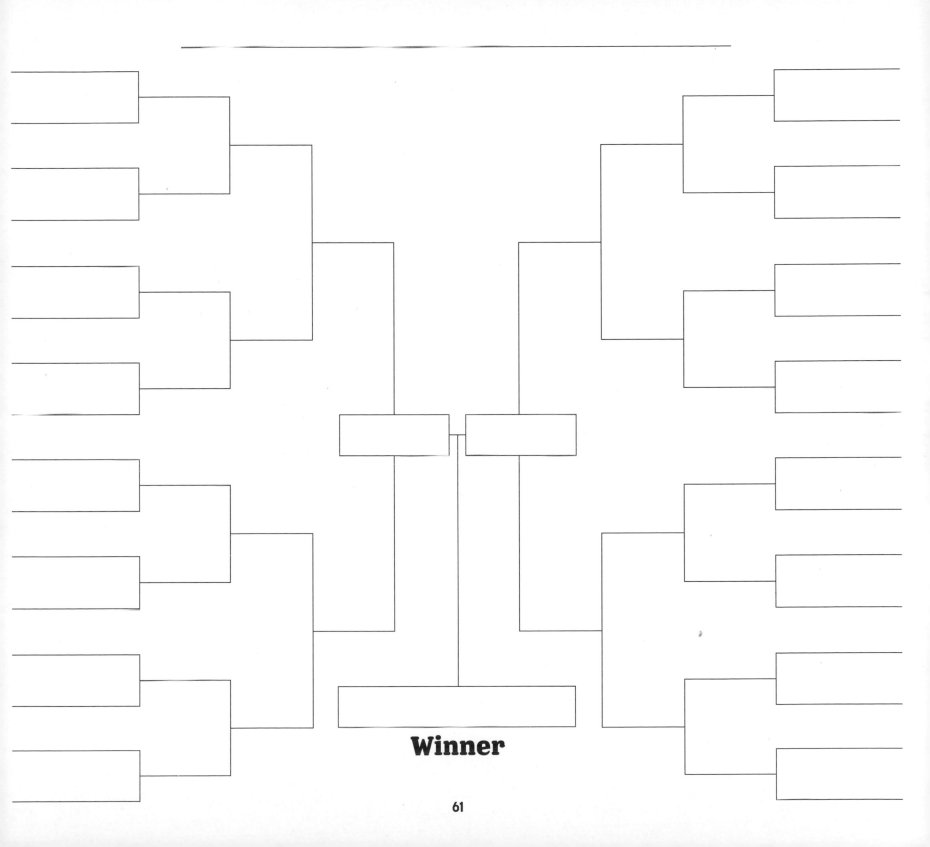

Winner

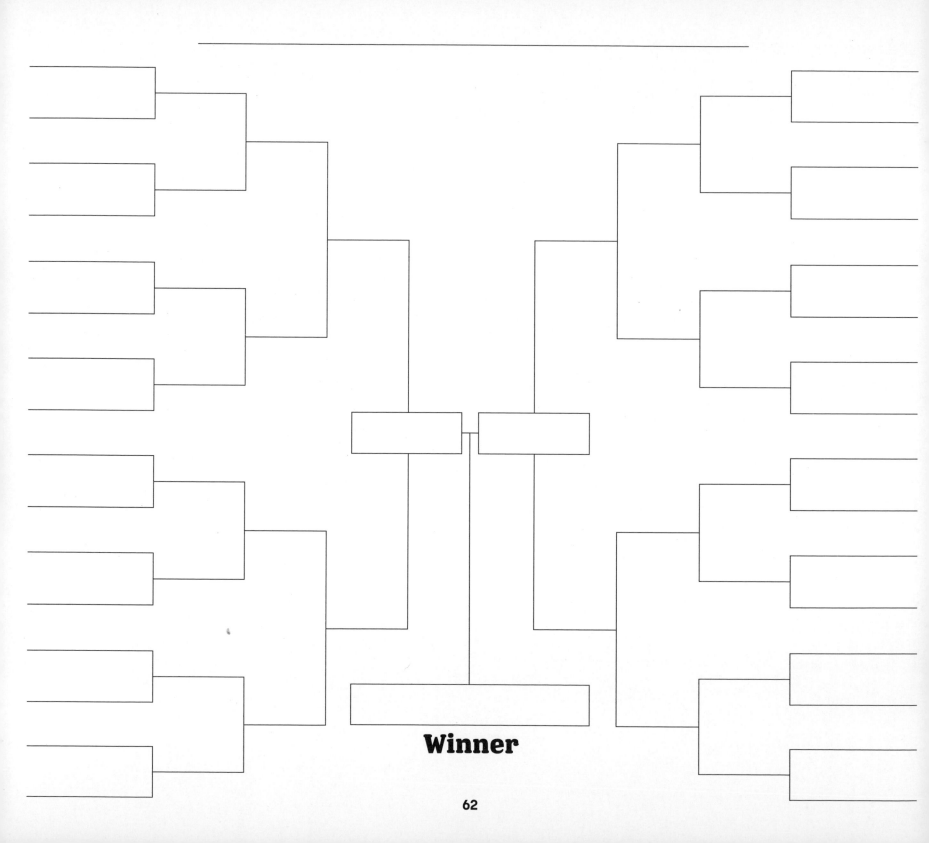

Winner

Winner

Winner